Coyotes

Victoria Blakemore

vblakemore.author@gmail.com

Copyright info/picture credits

Cover, skeeze/Pixabay; Page 3, skeeze/Pixabay; Page 5, skeeze/Pixabay; Page 7, ReverandRubbish/Pixabay; Page 9, Falkenpost/Pixabay; Pages 10-11, Storyblocks; Page 13, skeeze/Pixabay; Page 15, skeeze/Pixabay; Page 17, skeeze/Pixabay; Page 19, DrReyesFournier/Pixabay; Page 21, Martha Marks/AdobeStock; Page 23; DrillingEngineer/Pixabay; Page 25, jl1262/Pixabay; Page 27, tpsdave/Pixabay; Page 29, skeeze/Pixabay; Page 31, tpsdave/Pixabay; Page 33, skeeze/Pixabay

Table of Contents

What Are Coyotes?

Coyotes are large mammals. They are members of the same family as dogs and wolves.

There are about twenty different kinds of coyotes. They differ in color, size, and where they live.

They have fur that is a mix of white, beige, gray, and black. This helps them to blend in to their habitat.

Size

Coyotes are usually about three feet long. Their tail is at least twelve inches long.

Coyotes are smaller than some members of the dog family. They usually weigh between twenty and fifty pounds.

Male coyotes are usually

larger than female coyotes.

Coyotes and wolves are very similar. They are often hard to tell apart. One difference is that coyotes have a longer, thinner snout.

Coyotes have a very thick coat of fur. It helps to keep them warm in the winter.

Coyotes have large, pointed ears. This helps them to have a good sense of hearing. They can hear prey from far away.

Habitat

Coyotes usually live in deserts, prairies, and forests. They may also be found in the mountains.

Coyotes are very smart and have been known to **adapt** to life in areas where people live.

Range

Coyotes are found in North

and Central America.

They are found in every state except Hawaii. They are also found in Canada and Mexico. II

Diet

Coyotes are **omnivores**. They eat both meat and plants.

Their diet is made up of small mammals such as rabbits, squirrels, and rats. They may also eat plants like cactus flowers.

Coyotes have been seen

bringing food they have caught

to injured or sick coyotes.

Coyotes may hunt in groups, but have also been seen hunting alone if their prey is small.

Coyotes are **scavengers**. They often eat pieces of prey leftover from other predators, such as wolves.

When hunting, coyotes may pounce on their prey to catch it.

Communication

Coyotes use sound, scent, and movement to communicate with other coyotes.

They have a special scent that they use to mark their **territory**. Certain **postures** can be used to show how a coyote is feeling.

Coyotes use sounds like growls, yelps, barks, and howls to communicate.

Movement

Coyotes are faster than many other members of the dog family. They have been known to run up to forty-three miles per hour.

Just like dogs, coyotes use panting to make sure they don't get overheated.

Coyotes can also jump long

distances when chasing prey.

They can jump over ten feet.

Coyote Pups

Coyotes usually have a litter of between five and seven babies in the spring. The babies are called pups.

The pups are born in a den that is underground or in the bushes. Both parents help to take care of them.

The father hunts and brings food back to the den while the mother protects the pups from predators.

Pack Life

Most coyotes live in groups that are called packs. They are led by a pair of coyotes called the **alphas**.

Packs live in large dens that they often dig into a hillside. Their dens are full of tunnels and **chambers**.

Coyotes are usually most active

at **dawn** and **dusk**.

Lifespan

In the wild, many coyotes live

between six and eight years.

They have been known to live

as long as fourteen years.

Coyotes can become sick or

be infested with **parasites**.

They are sometimes hunted

by humans.

Coyotes that live in **captivity** often live longer than wild coyotes. This is because they have plenty of food and care if they get sick.

Population

Coyotes are not **endangered**.
In fact, coyote populations in
the wild are very high.

Large coyote populations can
be a problem. They may prey
on **livestock**, which makes
many people think of them as
pests.

People are trying to manage
coyote populations through
hunting and trapping.

Keystone Species

Coyotes are a **keystone species**. They are important to their ecosystem. Many other species need coyotes.

Coyotes keep the populations of animals like raccoons, opossums, and foxes from getting too large. This helps the populations of other species.

If coyotes did not keep smaller

predator populations from getting

too big, other species would suffer.

Helping Coyotes

People have been trying to control coyote populations for many years. They have used hunting and trapping to keep populations low.

When coyotes are hunted for population control, more coyotes are born. Their populations actually increases.

Some researchers are saying that we should leave coyotes alone. They say that coyote populations will not get too big if they are left alone.

Researchers are still studying coyotes. They want to learn more about how they help their ecosystem and how we can help them.

Glossary

Adapt: to change, adjust

Alpha: the animal that is in charge of a group

Captivity: animals that are kept by humans, not in the wild

Chamber: room

Dawn: the time in the morning when the sun starts to rise

Dusk: the time in the evening when the sun starts to go down

Endangered: at risk of becoming extinct

Keystone Species: a species that is necessary for the survival of the ecosystem

Livestock: animals that are kept on farms

Omnivore: an animal that eats meat and plants

Parasite: a plant, fungus, or animal that feeds off of another creature

Posture: body position

Scavenger: an animal that eats another animal's leftovers

Territory: an area of land that an animal claims as its own

About the Author

Victoria Blakemore is a first grade

teacher in Southwest Florida with a

passion for reading.

You can visit her at

www.elementaryexplorers.com

Also in This Series

Gray Wolves	Sloths	Flamingos	Camels	Koalas	Honey Bees	Pandas
Pangolins	White-Tailed Deer	Orcas	Giraffes	Corn	Meerkats	Echidnas
Walruses	Raccoons	Bald Eagles	Apples	Arctic Foxes	Red Pandas	Cassowaries
Tigers	Ladybugs	Moose	Beluga Whales	Leopards	Elephants	Jellyfish
Binturongs	Lions	Dolphins	Reindeer	Hammerhead Sharks	Hippos	Pumpkins
Peafowl	Chameleons	Florida Panthers	Aye-Ayes	Black Bears	Cheetahs	Manatees
Gingerbread	Polar Bears	Hot Chocolate	Orangutans	Coyotes	Marshmallows	Strawberries

All titles by Victoria Blakemore

Also in This Series

Aardvarks	Mako Sharks	Alligators	Frogs	Hedgehogs	Brown Bears	Bongos
Sea Turtles	Quokkas	Muskrats	Zebras	Red Foxes	Ring-Tailed Lemurs	Platypuses
Anteaters	Kangaroos	Rhinos	Jaguars	Wombats	Capybaras	Gorillas
Cats	Skunks	Butterflies	Dingoes	Snow Leopards	African Wild Dogs	Penguins
Whale Sharks	Wolverines	Warthogs	Caracals	Badgers	Seals	Hummingbirds
Pikas	Humpback Whales	Pumas	Lemonade	Llamas	Tulips	Ostriches
Sunflowers	Fennec Foxes	Sea Lions	Squirrels	Roses	Porcupines	Ice Cream

Victoria Blakemore

www.ingramcontent.com/pod-product-compliance
Lightning Source LLC
Chambersburg PA
CBHW051251020426
42333CB00025B/3157